Table of Contents

Introduction

I am a mother to an 18-month-old toddler. I researched a lot of activities for my child that would help her develop and that would also be fun. I combined activities that I found in different resources into one bundle, added some of our own activities and I'm sharing these activities with other moms that don't have time to do extensive research. All the activities in the book have been tested on our toddler, and I only included those that she liked. The target group for these activities is 12 to 18-month-old toddlers, but I think 18 to 24-month-olds would enjoy them as well. All kids are different though, and if your child is not interested in some activities, try them again later. Kids develop and change their interests so fast!
Also, feel free to visit my blog at www.chicklink.com where I share some of the activities as our child grows.

Some of the activities in this book require the use of the printable files. All files can be downloaded from www.chicklink.com/65-activities-printables.

Disclaimer

Please supervise your children for all the activities described in this book, especially since toddlers of this age are very inclined in putting everything in their mouths. Some of the activities in the book recommend using small objects that can pose choking hazards for children, use these objects extra carefully and with strong supervision, or skip the activity. Hope you find some activities that your child enjoys!

Monochrome color tray

Category: Montessori-inspired, sensory play

Materials: objects of one color, tray.

The sensory tray is a great way for a toddler to interact with and learn about objects. Trays can be categorized by color, shape, texture, purpose, and theme. In order to get your toddler familiarized with colors, psychologists recommend to start introducing primary colors first: yellow, red and blue, then add secondary colors: green, purple and orange. Look for any objects in your house of the same color that could be interesting to your toddler but safe to play with. It's best to collect objects of different textures and sizes. Some ideas are: kitchen items, duplo blocks, books, construction paper, thread rolls, toys, balls, large straws, and plastic cups. Make sure to watch your child carefully if you are using small objects.

Benefits: development of the concept of color, sensory enrichment, discovery and motor skills.

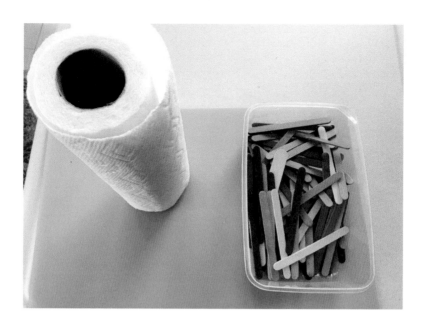

Craft sticks drop

Category: sorting activities

Materials: colored craft sticks, paper towel roll.

Craft sticks are so colorful that I couldn't miss an opportunity to use them for some activity. Because our toddler loves to drop things, we made another dropping activity. Put either a paper towel roll or a cardboard tube in front of your toddler and show how to drop craft sticks there.

Benefits: hand eye coordination, grasping skills.

Action cards

Category: physical development, intellectual development

Materials: printable files, laminating sheets(optional).

Download action cards from http://chicklink.com/65-activities-printables. There is a total of 8 cards: 4 animal actions and 4 objects actions. Show one action card to your toddler at a time, read it, and show how to perform the action. Encourage him or her to repeat after you. The simplest actions have been selected to be appropriate for this age group.

Benefits: gross motor skills, object recognition, improvement of body control, poise, balance and coordination.

Spices sensory play

Category: sensory play, Montessori-inspired
Materials: spices, tray.

A tray of spices can be great sensory play for your toddler. It's best to use spices that don't have sharp flavors (like peppers), since you can open, smell, and touch some of them. Your toddler will enjoy shaking them, checking the sounds that different bottles make, taking some of them out, and just exploring and observing them. This is also a great activity to do when you need to get something done in the kitchen and your toddler needs to be entertained. Make sure to watch your child not to develop any allergies when interacting with spices.

Benefits: develops senses of smell, touch, taste, hearing, understanding of rhythm, and great for overall sensory awareness.

Find the sound

Category: physical development

Materials: sound-making toy.

Probably all kids have a toy that plays music when you press a button. If your toddler is a good walker, hide the toy anywhere in the house and press the button so it starts making noise. Ask your toddler to find the toy by following the sound. It's better if the music is playing for a while so a child has time to listen to it and find the toy. If your toddler is not walking yet, you can hide the toy in the room where it can be accessed by crawling. If you don't have a toy that makes noise, you can use an alarm clock.

Benefits: gross motor skills, discovery skills, sensory processing and exploration.

Musical tray

Category: skill development

Materials: musical instruments, empty bottles, pans, spoons.

It's good to develop your child's musical skills as early as possible. Collect any musical instruments you have and arrange them on a tray. If you don't have any, use empty plastic bottles filled with things that rattle: rice, beans, pasta (make sure to seal the bottle cap with hot glue for safety). It's easy to make drums out of a pot and 2 spoons. Wooden spoons, bells, and shakers can all be used for rhythm development. Singing, humming, and clapping hands to the beat and dancing is highly encouraged. It's also great to let your child listen to different types of music. Create playlists of different genres: jazz, flamenco, classical, polka, or rock and see which style your child prefers. You can also teach your child to recognize the instruments that are being played.

Benefits: development of rhythm, pitch and melody.

Straw pieces sorter

Category: sorting activities

Materials: empty bottle, large straws.

Bottles can be used for all kinds of sorting activities. For younger toddlers, it's better to use a bottle with a wider mouth. Large straws are also great for sorting. Cut them in pieces large enough not to fit in a toddler's mouth. Drinking straw pieces are easy for toddlers to handle and manipulate, they are also usually a bright color and will make rattling sounds when placed in a bottle. Show your toddler how to put them in a bottle one by one, and take them out of the bottle by turning it upside down. Make sure to watch your child not to put straw pieces in the mouth. Sometimes we put blueberries in a bottle instead of straw pieces. Because our child is a peaky eater, I try to come up with activities that use food for playing.

Benefits: fine motor skills, hand eye coordination, grasping, development of concept of size and shape.

Bingo

Category: intellectual development

Materials: printable files, laminating sheets(optional).

You can download the cards to play the bingo game from http://chicklink.com/65-activities-printables. The set includes black and white images of animals and their color copies. Put the letter size sheet with black and white images on the table. Cut out the color images of the animals to get 4 cards. You can laminate them for durability. Give one color card to the child and ask him or her to find the same image in black and white - then show how to cover that image with color version. Continue until all black and white images are covered with the colored version.

Benefits: object recognition, learning names of animals, gaining control over hand movements.

Color paper pieces on a window

Category: creativity development

Materials: construction paper, water.

Cut out random shapes from construction paper. Place the paper shapes in a bowl of water for a moment. Encourage your toddler to place it on a window or mirror. The shapes look very colorful and bright once they are spread on a surface. This activity is great for learning shape names as well. Paper will fall off when dry.

Benefits: fine motor skills, pincer grip, learning shape names.

Notes: Do this using brightly coloured & monochrome postcards & photos onto garden doors with bluetac

Paper window

Category: intellectual development

Materials: a folder or piece of cardboard and a book.

Here is another discovery game. All you need is an empty folder and a book. Cut folder in half and cut out a square or round opening. You can use a sheet of cardboard or paper as well. Place it on a book with illustrations and move it around to discover images.

Benefits: discovery skills, focusing on one object, learning new vocabulary.

Nested Objects

Category: skill development, Montessori-inspired

Materials: nesting dolls/ nesting cups/ measuring cups/ boxes of different size.

The best toy for this activity is a set of nesting dolls, but you can also use different size boxes and hide one inside the other. A set of nesting cups or a set of measuring cups also works well. Our toddler really enjoys assembling and disassembling them. It's a great activity for learning the concept of big and small, learning to open boxes or nesting dolls, and for trying to fit things inside other things. Our toddler plays a lot with nesting dolls by shaking them, taking them apart, assembling them, carrying them around the house, and pointing to their eyes, mouth and nose.

Benefits: object permanence, concept of big and small, fine motor skills, learning to make comparisons between objects.

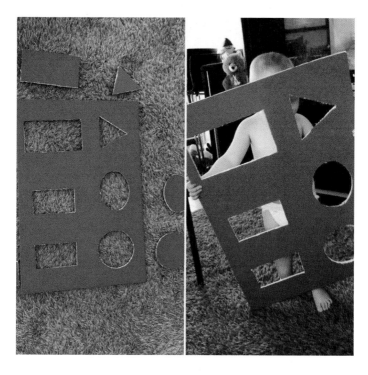

Peek-a-boo board

Category: skill development, physical development

Materials: foam board/cardboard.

I got an idea for this activity from going to a playground, when our toddler was playing peek-a-boo from behind a fence. I decided to make a big board with openings in it so she would peek through them when we are at home. Take a foam board or cardboard and cut out a few openings of any shapes you like. You can take turns playing peek-a-boo with your baby. You can save this board and shapes that you cut out for later, when it can be used as a giant shape sorter.

Benefits: discovery skills, gross motor skills, learning shapes.

Toys inside boxes

Category: skill development

Materials: boxes, toys.

Toddlers love to discover things, so this makes for a great discovery game. For this activity, look for boxes around your house that have different closing mechanisms, and put a toy in each one. It's better not to use more than 3 or 4 boxes. Encourage your baby to open a box to find the toy inside. You can shake the box or open it to show that there is something inside to get the child interested. Once the toy is found, you can name the toy that was found and talk about it. We use a jewelry box, a tin box and a gift box. We usually use animal figures for hiding, that way we get to learn the animal names and the sounds they make. When a toy is found, we put another one in a box, so this activity can be repeated as long as the child is interested.

Benefits: motor skills development, discovery skills, learning new words, teaching object permanence.

18

Velcro strips practice

Category: Montessori-inspired

Materials: cardboard, velcro strips, hot glue.

This activity was inspired by Montessori tablets that teach self-care skills. Maria Montessori described tablets for development of dressing and undressing. Learning how to fasten velcro is one of these skills. We made a tablet from a piece of cardboard. Then we used hot glue to attach one side of 4 strips to the board, and left the 4 other strips unattached. Show your toddler how to fasten the strips and take them off. Our toddler was more interested in taking them off.

Benefits: self-care skills, hand eye coordination.

Fruit and water play

Category: sensory play, Montessori-inspired

Materials: fruits, water, cups, plates.

The setup is easy, just cut some apples and oranges and add water! Toddlers love playing with water, especially if there is something interesting they can find in the water. You can also give your child a cup, a plate, and a fork from a play set and show how to get fruits out of the water with a fork (or hand) and put it on a plate. You can also show how to get water in a cup and drink it. Self care is one of the main principles of Montessori education, and learning how to drink yourself and serve yourself food are the first goals Maria Montessori recommends achieving. The benefit for us was our very picky eater ate some apples that she got out of the water!

Benefits: self-care skills, learning independence, sensory awareness, learning fruit names.

Hide the toy

Category: physical development

Materials: toys, a blanket.

This activity is so easy, it can be played anytime, and is always a hit. Hide a toy underneath a tablecloth or blanket and ask your toddler to find it. When the toy is found, hide another one. This activity can last as long as you want it to. This game is great for learning toy names and for teaching object permanence. Our toddler loves this game, she brings me a tablecloth to show that she wants to play.

Benefits: object permanence, vocabulary development, discovery skills.

Learning words with flashcards

Category: intellectual development

Materials: flashcards, objects shown on flashcards.

This activity is based on the Glenn Doman technique for teaching your baby to read. His technique involves showing 5 flash cards at a time to your baby 3 times a day for a few seconds. It's better if cards have images of an object, not illustrations, so it's easier for your child to identify them. You can start this activity as early as possible. Doman recommends flash cards from as early as 3 months. We do this activity a bit differently. We try to find the pictured object at home, if we have it, we place it next to the card. We also take our time looking at the cards, we read them, play with objects and then ask our toddler if she can point to the object.

One of the other supporters of flash card reading is Professor Makoto Shichida, who wrote many books about techniques to stimulate early development of the brain. According to him, all babies between 0 and 3 years old have mental abilities of a gifted child. He splits development into right brain and left brain development. As you know, left brain controls things like logic, written and spoken languages, scientific ability and number skills. The Shichida method targets the development of the right brain which is responsible for the photographic memory ability, computer-like calculation ability, intuition and creative imagination. All these skills can be acquired by doing exercises that stimulate the right brain.

One of these exercises is speed reading of flash cards - flash cards need to be shown to your child at a fast speed. It develops the right brain's imaging activity by inputting massive amounts of information as fast as possible. The left brain works at low speed rhythm while the right brain works at high speed rhythm. When massive information is input at a high speed, the right brain responds to it naturally and imaging capability is developed. As a result, when you try to remember something, an image will appear in your brain, containing the information. Since the flashing of the cards is happening very fast, the left brain doesn't have enough time to process it and that's when right brain gets involved getting the stimulation needed to activate its powers. Prime time for card flashing is 0 to 3 years.

I read a book by Makoto Shichida, and wrote the overview of his principles in an article at http://chicklink.com/shichida-method, if anyone is interested to read details.

Benefits: language development, literacy skills, sensory processing.

Sticky note peek-a-boo

Category: intellectual development

Materials: a book, sticky notes.

Any book can become suddenly more interesting when you add sticky notes to it. You can add sticky notes to any book to create flaps. You can either place sticky notes on animal illustrations in a book in advance, or you can do this as you read the book. We place sticky notes on the animal images as we read, and our toddler still gets excited when she takes the sticky note off to discover the animal underneath. Sticky notes can be placed on any illustration in a book that would be fun for a child to discover.

Benefits: discovery skills, pincer grip, language and communication.

Foil wrapped toys

Category: skill development

Materials: aluminum foil, toys.

Wrap some toys in aluminum foil and let your child unwrap them. We wrap animal toys in foil, and once each toy is discovered, we repeat the animal's name and the sound it makes. As an option, foil wrapped toys can also be hidden in a bin of rice so the child can discover them. This is one of our toddler's favorite activities. You can make this activity last as long as the child is interested by rewrapping toys that have been already opened. If you are using small toys, make sure to watch your child carefully during this activity.

Benefits: fine motor skills, language development, discovery skills.

Magnetic theater

Category: intellectual development

Materials: printable file, magnetic sheets, baking tray.

You can bring any story to life by setting up a magnetic theater. You just need to find a story that doesn't have too many or too few characters. We made a magnetic theater for the nursery rhyme "5 little ducks". You can download a printable file with illustrations from www.chicklink.com/65-activities-printables. You will need a couple of magnetic sheets, the illustrations, and a baking tray. Place the images on the adhesive magnetic sheets, cut them out, and stick magnetic ducks on the baking tray. This song has a great melody and it's also good for learning numbers. Now you can do the actions as the song goes by removing one little duck from the baking tray at a time. Our toddler also carried the ducks around and put them on our fridge door.

Benefits: motor skills, musical skills, creativity development.

Reading time props

Category: intellectual development

Materials: a book, animal toys.

Whenever you read a book to your child, support book images with toys you have around. You can set this up in advance: collect toys appearing in the book and reveal them as the story goes. You can make toys jump around, talk, tickle your baby, or do actions described in the book.

Benefits: concept recognition, sensory processing, literacy skills.

Bowling

Category: physical development

Materials: empty bottles, balls.

Bowling is fun for the whole family. You can set it up at home by using a few empty bottles and different size balls. You can show your toddler that if you roll a bigger ball, it would knock down more bottles, and if you roll a small ball, it might hit just one bottle. This activity is great for a toddler to learn to coordination.

Benefits: gross motor skills, a concept of big and small skills for measuring distance, precision.

The cups game

Category: skill development

Materials: cups, small toy.

Cups game is a great way to entertain your child, and it's easy to set up. All you need is 3 or 4 cups and a small toy. Hide a toy underneath one of the cups and shuffle them. Encourage your child to look for the toy. The game teaches object permanence (the toy doesn't disappear when it's hidden) and it's just fun to play! We always clap our hands when our toddler finds a toy, which makes the activity even more exciting for her. Make sure to watch your child extra carefully because this activity involves playing with a small toy.

Benefits: object permanence, grasping skills.

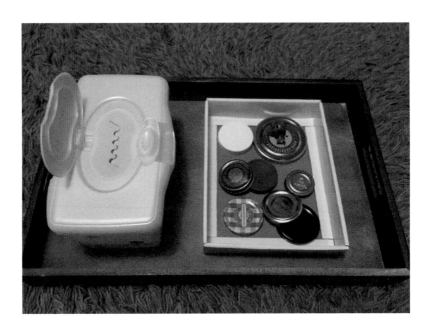

Lid sorter

Category: sorting activities

Materials: a wipes box, jar lids.

Jar lids are great for sorting activities because they are large enough not to fit in the child's mouth, and they are easy to grasp and manipulate for little hands. Boxes from wipes are also ideal for sorting because their opening is big enough to fit lids and has soft edges. Show your child that you need to put lids inside the opening of the box, and show how you can open the box after and find all the lids inside. We clap after each lid makes it in, and our toddler gets more motivated and excited.

Benefits: fine motor skills, hand eye coordination, object permanence, development of concept of size and shape.

Strainer fun

Category: sorting activity

Materials: strainer, zip-ties/q-tips/thin straws.

You probably have supplies for this activity at home. Put a strainer in front of your child, and show how to put zip-ties in the gaps and how to take them out. Instead of zip-ties you can also use q-tips, thin straws, or pipe cleaners, depending on how big the gaps in the strainer are.

Benefits: fine motor skills, precision skills, hand eye coordination.

Lid matching

Category: skill development, Montessori-inspired

Materials: empty bottles, bottle lids.

This is an easy to set up activity that your toddler will probably enjoy. All you need is a couple of empty plastic bottles and lids. It's tough for little hands to put a lid on a bottle, they might need a lot of practice. It gets more challenging when there are lids of different sizes and they need to pick the right one. At a younger age, you can give your toddler just one bottle and a lid, so they can practice putting the lid on and taking it off. For toddlers a bit older, you can offer 2 or 3 bottles to introduce the challenge of matching the lid to the correct size bottle. I tried to find a bottle with a bigger mouth so the lid wouldn't be too small. If you are using bottles with small lids, make sure to watch your child extra carefully.

Benefits: development of fine motor skills, grasping skills, shape and size recognition.

Animal of the day

Category: intellectual development

Materials: toys and books.

It's easier for a child to understand information one concept at a time. You can use this principle to teach anything, but we use it to learn about animals because kids are so interested in animals at this age. Pick one animal a day, and try to find references to that animal in your house. Look through your toddler's books together and point to each occurrence of that animal. Find a stuffed animal or animal toy (if you have it), or watch a short video about it. Learn animal sounds, and perhaps some actions that animal does.

Benefits: language development, literacy development, object recognition.

Help around the house

Category: Montessori-inspired, skill development

You can include your toddler in your everyday day activities. Kids love to copy everything we do, and it's a great way for them to learn how things are done, to learn new vocabulary, to have new sensory experiences. All you need is some patience because with your toddler's help, the chores might take twice longer. Some things that we do together:

- Sweeping floors. I even got her a little broom to help out.
- Dusting shelves. It's the cutest thing to see her with a duster.
- Cooking. We use a learning tower that has been a great help for us, but you can use a bassinet, high chair or a sling. Our toddler loves to explore vegetables, help me wash things, whisk water in a bowel, watch me prepare things. It can get messy but it's worth it.

Benefits: development of independence, fine motor skills, sensory training.

Drawing inside the box

Category: creativity development

Materials: large cardboard box, pencils.

Kids are a bit like cats. They like boxes. A great way to entertain your child is to let them get inside a box with pencils, markers or finger paint and create art inside the box.

Benefits: creativity, imagination and motor skills.

Pompoms and cupcake liners play

Category: sensory play

Materials: pompoms, cupcake liners.

Sometimes it doesn't take much to entertain a child. Because pompoms are so bright and colorful they are capable to keep a toddler engaged for a while. Cupcake liners can be a good addition for pompom play. You can show your toddler to put a pompom in each one. Later, when your child can sort by colors, you can use cupcake liners for sorting pompoms to match their color. Usually kids can sort by colors when they are over 18 months old. Our toddler was very interested in this activity, she put pompoms in mini cupcake liners, took them out, and rearranged them. This activity should be supervised to make sure your child doesn't put pompoms in his or her mouth.

Benefits: development of sensory awareness, hand eye coordination.

Matching lids to jars

Category: skill development

Materials: a printable file, empty puree jars, a box.

This activity comes with a printable drawing that can be downloaded from http://chicklink.com/65-activities-printables. Tape or glue a drawing to a box, and cut out openings in the place of the circles. Insert puree jars into the box and give lids to the baby to put on the jars. The game can be used for older toddlers as well, if you paint the lids with colors to match the drawing. Our toddler loves this activity. Taking lids off and putting them back on seems to keep her busy. You can also offer pompoms or cotton balls to your toddler to put in and out of the jars.

Benefits: motor skills, sensory processing and color recognition.

Matching toys to pictures

Category: intellectual development

Materials: toys, images of toys.

This activity requires some prep time. You need to take pictures of some toys and have them printed in advance. There are a few games you can play with these pictures later. The simplest one is to ask the toddler to match the picture to a toy. It's a good way to learn the names of animals. You can also arrange toys in the room, show the picture of the toy, and ask your toddler to bring it to you. Another option is to put the toys in a box, show the picture to your child, say the name of the animal, and ask him or her to find this toy. Later, when a toddler is over 2 years old, you can put toys in a bag, show a picture of the toy, and have your child find the toy without looking in the bag.

Benefits: sensory processing and exploration skills, object recognition, vocabulary development.

Colored rice play

Category: sensory play, Montessori-inspired

Materials: rice, small toys/ funnel/ containers/ cups.

Rice play is a great sensory activity. While you can use white rice, kids really love colored rice, so I think it's worth taking the time to color it. Here are some ideas of how to play:

- Transfer rice from one container to another.
- Hide toys in rice and look for them.
- Walk on the rice.
- Make rice tea by filling a play teapot with rice and filling cups with it. This rice tea can be served to toys and dolls.
- Make rice rain. Make rice fall from your hand from a low height, kids usually love to watch it fall. Just make sure to put a sheet underneath for easy cleanup.
- Pour rice through a funnel.

Benefits: gross motor skills, fine motor skills, creativity, imagination.

Learning emotions

Category: intellectual development

Materials: printable file/ paper and markers.

This activity serves the purpose of introducing emotions to your toddler. You can either make it yourself or download a printable file of emotion faces from www.chicklink.com/65-activities-printables. If you are doing it yourself, cut out 4 circles from paper, and then draw a happy, a sad, an angry, and a surprised face. Glue them or tape them together. Show each face to your toddler, simultaneously making this face yourself. Toddlers copy everything we do, so soon you'll see your little one trying to make the faces, and it's the cutest thing.

Benefits: learning about emotions, coordination of facial muscles.

Finger painting

Category: creativity development

Materials: finger paint, paper, q-tips/ brushes.

There are a variety of paints to use for finger painting. You can buy them or make them yourself by mixing yogurt or sour cream with food coloring. We use organic food coloring in the event our toddler decides to taste it. Applesauce can also be used as a painting medium. Here are some painting ideas:

- Leave circle marks by dipping paper towel rolls in paint.
- Tape a large piece of wrapping paper to the floor, white side up. Let your child paint all over it.
- Paint by dipping animal toy's feet in paint and leave footmarks on paper.
- Paint with brushes or q-tips.

Benefits: creativity, imagination, fine motor skills, gross motor skills, hand coordination.

Flash cards in envelopes

Category: skill development, intellectual development

Materials: envelopes, flash cards.

Put flash cards in envelopes for your toddler to open. This activity is good for learning to handle objects and for concentrating attention on one card. Every time your toddler gets a card out of the envelope, say the name of the object on the card. It's best to use flashcards that have images of objects, not illustrations, in order for your child to easier understand what it is.

Benefits: learning to handle envelopes, learning new vocabulary.

Ping pong sorter

Category: sorting activities

Materials: ping pong balls, container.

Cut out an opening in a container slightly larger than the size of a ping pong ball (it's hard to see the opening in this picture because the lid is clear). A toddler's task is to get a ball in the container using ice cream scooper. Younger toddlers can use their hands instead of a scooper.

Benefits: hand eye coordination, gaining control over hand movements.

Shapes sensory play

Category: sensory play, Montessori-inspired

Materials: rice, shapes.

You can make a sensory bin out of rice and different shapes you have around - perhaps you have some cookie cutters, cubes or shapes from a sorting toy. Hide them in rice, and help your child discover them. Upon discovery, take your child's finger and follow the shape's edge in the same direction as if you would draw the shape. This is what Maria Montessori refers to as a stereognostic sense in "Dr. Montessori's Own Handbook". She says that stereognostic sense is the capacity to recognize forms by the movement of the muscles of the hand as it follows the outlines of solid objects. Perception of form comes from the combination of two sensations, tactile and muscular, muscular sensations being sensations of movement.

Benefits: perception of form, preparing child's hand for drawing in the future, sensory awareness.

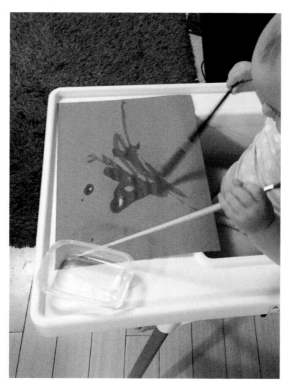

Paint with water

Category: creativity development

Materials: construction paper, water.

All you need is construction paper and water – super easy to set up and clean up. Show your toddler how to leave marks on paper with a finger. Our toddler likes to use a brush, but some kids prefer to paint with fingers or sponges.

Benefits: development of creativity, sensory awareness, fine motors skills.

Ping pong toss

Category: sorting activities

Materials: ping pong balls, box.

You need a set of balls and an empty box for this activity. We used ping pong balls, but any balls would work. The goal is to throw them into the box. We've been using our cardboard house for this activity. Every toddler likes to throw things, but this game can show them how to throw with a purpose, how to coordinate movement and direct balls in one direction. The whole family can participate.

Benefits: hand eye coordination, gross motor skills and fun for the whole family!

Pompoms sorter

Category: sorting activity

Materials: tissue box, pompoms.

You can turn a tissue box into a hungry animal by either printing an image of an animal's face or by drawing it on a box. Tissue boxes are perfect for sorting activities because it's easy to get things out of them through the tissue feeder. You can download an image of a tiger that would fit a standard tissue box size from www.chicklink.com/65-activities-printables. Glue or tape it to a box, cut out the mouth area for the size of the feeding material, and your tiger is ready to eat. You can use pompoms or cotton balls for feeding. Make sure to watch that your child does not put pompoms in his or her mouth.

Benefits: fine motor skills, hand eye coordination, grasping, development of concept of size and shape, object permanence.

Draw on an edible sand

Category: sensory play

Materials: cream of wheat, tray.

You don't need to wait for summer to play with sand. Little artists can express themselves by drawing on a layer of cream of wheat on a tray. Besides drawing with fingers, you can also show your toddler how to draw with a q-tip or a craft stick. Cookie cutters can also be used for leaving shape marks.

Benefits: creativity development, sensory training.

Tissue paper play

Category: sensory play

Materials: tissue paper, animal toys.

Tear up tissue paper into small pieces and hide animal toys underneath. When your toddler finds each one, you can repeat animal names and sounds they make, or do a tickle attack. This is a great sensory activity and it helps language development if you talk about items you find.

Benefits: sensory awareness, discovery skills, vocabulary development.

The chicken dance

Category: physical development

Materials: chicken dance music or video.

Learning a chicken dance is a fun activity for the whole family. We usually turn on a video of other kids doing the dance on youtube and join the dance. It's a fun activity as it teaches kids to recognize the rhythm and follow it with movements of arms and feet. The biggest benefit, of course, is watching your child doing adorable dance moves.

Benefits: gross motor skills, development of music skills, recognizing rhythm and melody.

Manipulating zippers

Category: Montessori-inspired, skill development

Materials: bags that have zippers, toys.

This activity will prepare your child for the important skills of self-dressing and undressing. Self-care is one of the most important skills of Montessori education - teaching children to be independent. Take a few small bags that have zippers and place toys inside them. Show your child that there is a toy inside a bag and help to unzip it. Little by little, a child will get better hand control and will be able to do it independently.

Benefits: fine motor skills, development of self-care skills, learning names of toys hidden inside a bag, discovery skills.

Ice play

Category: sensory play

Materials: ice cube tray, small animal toys/a teapot.

Ice play is a great way for toddlers to be introduced to a little science experiment by watching it melt. You can either make water ice cubes or freeze animal toys in an ice cube tray and give the ice cubes to your toddler for exploration. You can also show how ice will melt by pouring warm water over it using a little teapot, a pipette, or a cup. If you are using small toys, make sure to supervise your child during this activity.

Benefits: discovery skills, sensory processing, concept of warm and cold, understanding of the world, cause and effect.

Cards drop

Category: sorting activity

Materials: container, cards.

Get any container that would fit the cards. We use a large yogurt container, but containers from Quaker Oats work great too. Cut out an opening in the lid and show your toddler how to put the cards in the container. I put tape on the edges of the opening to prevent our child from getting cut. I found cartoon playing cards that I decided to use for this activity, but any playing cards or other types of cards would work. The complexity of this activity can be increased if the opening is thinner.

Benefits: fine motor skills, hand eye coordination, grasping, development of concept of size and shape.

Ice pop play

Category: sensory play

Materials: ice pops, tray.

This is a great activity for educating young senses. It can introduce toddlers to the concept of cold/frozen, and they can learn about colors, length, and shape. This is a great vocabulary lesson if you talk about the qualities of ice pops. As children learn to connect words with objects, the world takes on a new meaning for them.

Benefits: sensory awareness, understanding of the world around us.

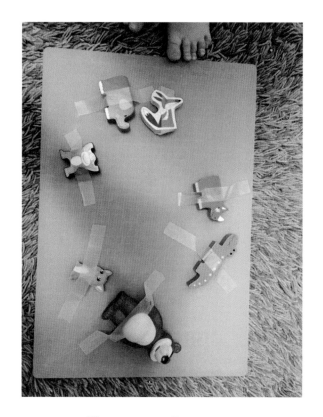

Rescue the toy

Category: physical development

Materials: toys, tape.

This activity is great for practicing pincer grip and fine motor skills. Tape a few toys to a table or a tray and encourage your toddler to pick up toys by removing tape from the surface. This activity can be played with older kids as well, they can pretend that they are saving toys from being captured by a villain. Make sure to watch your child carefully if you are using small toys.

Benefits: fine motor skills, pincer grip, learning animal names.

Old wallet play

Category: skill development

Materials: wallet, business cards/old credit cards/flashcards/playing cards.

Our toddler gets really excited when she finds my wallet, so I gave her my old wallet to explore and it had the same effect. Fill your old wallet with old credit cards, business cards, small flashcards, or playing cards. Arrange them in different compartments of the wallet, and perhaps, you can have a cup of coffee while your toddler takes the things out of the wallet.

Benefits: hand eye coordination, grasping skills, discovery skills.

Jelly sensory play

Category: sensory play

Materials: gelatin, juice.

Jelly play can be another interesting sensory activity for your child. The squishy and slippery texture of jelly is interesting indeed. You can use different containers and forms to make it. We decided to make a healthy version from the mixture of juice and water, in case our toddler would like to try it. The recipe is very simple: add 3 bags of gelatin to 1.5 cups of water, heat up 1.5 cups of juice and add it to the mixture. It takes about 5 minutes to prepare and 2 hours to cool. Then the mixture gets poured into mini cupcake tins. A few berries added to each slot can also be interesting to explore. After it's done, let your child touch it, try to cut it with plastic knife, taste it, and squish it.

Benefits: sensory awareness, development of senses of taste and smell.

Walking on sensory bags

Category: sensory play, Montessori-inspired

Materials: baby socks, grains.

Old baby socks can be turned into sensory bags. Fill them with beans, rice, pasta, cream of wheat, flour or any other grains. Your toddler will enjoy playing with them, touching them, throwing them, hiding them in boxes, or walking on them. If you make 2 of each sensory bags, later you can turn this activity into a classic Montessori activity, when a child has to match pairs by touching them with closed eyes.

Benefits: sensory awareness, sensory processing and recognition.

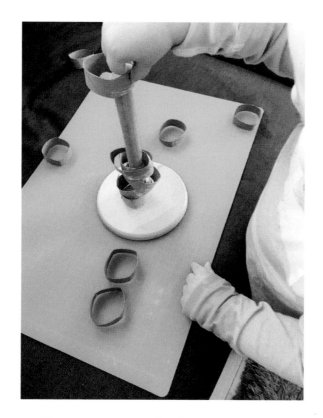

Paper towel circles play

Category: skill development

Materials: paper towel roll, paper towel/ stacking tower holder.

Cut paper towel tubes or toilet paper tubes into smaller circles, and show your toddler how to put circles on a paper towel holder or a stacking tower holder.

Benefits: fine motor skills, hand eye coordination.

Lint roller art

Category: creativity development

Materials: paper, lint roller, glitter/straw pieces/tissue paper pieces/ construction paper pieces.

Tape or glue a piece of lint roller sticky side up to a sheet of paper. Now your toddler can place anything to the sticky surface of the lint roller. We used pieces of straw, glitter, flower petals, tissue paper pieces, and glitter. We also drew on the paper around it with markers.

Benefits: creativity, sensory processing.

Plastic eggs play

Category: skill-development

Materials: plastic eggs, small toys.

You don't need to wait for Easter to play with plastic eggs. They can be bought online any time of the year, and provide a great playing material. Because of their bright colors, plastic eggs are very attractive for toddler to play with. There are numerous ways to play with them. One of the options is to hide small toys in some of the eggs, and mix them up with empty ones. Then encourage your toddler to pick up different eggs, and show him or her that the ones that produce sound have a toy inside them. The exercise provides a good practice for object manipulation. Our toddler gets excited when she finds a toy inside an egg. Another option how to play is to place eggs in an empty egg container using ice cream scoop or ladle. After a toddler turns 18 months, plastic eggs can be used for color sorting.

Benefits: learning the concept of empty and filled objects, hand eye coordination, discovery skills.

Water sensory bin

Category: sensory play, Montessori-inspired

Materials: container, water, cups/ lego blocks/ ice/ animal toys.

Probably all kids like to play with water. I don't add coloring to the water because our toddler plays with cups in the water and sometimes would drink the water from the cups. I don't stop her because it's a great self-care skill. But if a child is not interested in drinking, some blue food coloring can be added. Some ideas for water play include:

- make small plates float in the water and place small animals on them
- pour water from one container to another using a ladle or a small cup
- place different objects in the water and see which ones float and which ones do not (examples are sponge pieces, legos, flower petals, animal figures)
- add ice to water and watch it melt

Benefits: sensory processing, fine motor skills, concept of light and heavy.

Fridge time

Category: sensory play, Montessori-inspired

Materials: fridge.

In a Montessori home the child is allowed to explore the home naturally. One of the places where a toddler can find fascinating objects is the fridge. It's a great place for discovering objects, sensory play, and learning the names of food items. It's best to put glass bottles and glass jars up on higher shelves where your toddler can't reach them, and let them discover the rest. You'll be surprised how many objects your child will be interested in. Our toddler especially liked throwing potatoes on the floor and rolling limes around the house. This activity is great to feed your child's quest for discovery.

Benefits: learning names of food items, sensory and discovery play.

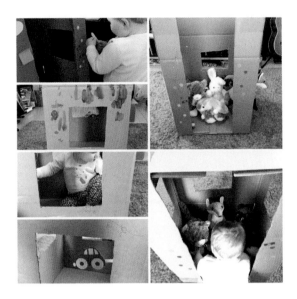

Cardboard house

Category: physical development

Materials: large box, stuffed animal toys/pencils/paint/stickers.

Boxes are very valuable when you have a toddler around. Convert it into a house by cutting out windows and a door. Here are some ideas on how to play with it:

- Peekaboo. You can reach through each window and tickle your toddler. Our toddler giggles and loves this playtime.
- Paint on it. You can paint on the house with a finger, hands, or a brush.
- Draw inside and outside the house.
- Make it a house for stuffed animals. This one seems to be the favorite activity of our toddler. She loves to bring stuffed animals to the house and then to take them out.
- Stickers. A house can be decorated with stickers.

Benefits: fine and gross motor skills, creativity development.

Paint Ziplock bag

Category: creative activities

Materials: Ziploc bag, paint.

A toddler can get artsy without getting messy. Place a few drops of paint of different colors in a Ziploc bag and let your child's curious hands explore. You can also tape the bag to a window so your child can stand next to it and see how the sunlight interacts with the paint. Show your child how to mix paints in the bag and create new colors.

Benefits: creativity, learning colors, sensory processing.

A sensory bottle

Category: sensory play

Materials: empty bottle, water, glitter/ beads/sand/buttons/sea shells/small animal toys.

Toddler play can include a variety of sensory or discovery bottles. You can use your creativity to put anything you like there. Some ideas include glitter, small animal toys, seashells, plastic letters, water beads, mini erasers, sand, beads, marbles, and buttons. You can add food coloring to the water to get a beautiful color, you can add hair gel for a slow-flow sensory bottle, or you can make it without liquid at all. You can make a themed discovery bottle, some ideas include: ocean life, animals, holidays, or nature. It's good to use hot glue to seal the bottle cap so the child would not be able to accidentally open it.

Benefits: discovery skills, object recognition, sensory processing and exploration.

Blowing activities

Materials: bubbles/a whistle/a paper butterfly/straw and a cup.

Blowing activities are very important for the development of oral motor skills as they teach the muscles to move in a specific way. These skills are very helpful for speech development. Oral motor skill exercises help develop strong and mobile articulators (lips, cheeks, jaw, and tongue). The ability to blow is essential for sound production. Here are some activities that help develop those skills:

- Blowing bubbles
- Blowing a whistle
- Blow in a straw in a cup of water to make bubbles
- Blow on a paper butterfly on a string to make it fly

Be careful to only do these activities for a little bit at a time - blowing for extended periods may cause dizziness.

Benefits: learning to coordinate lips, cheeks, and jaw, increased speech sound variety and improved speech clarity.

Q-tips drop

Category: sorting activity

Materials: q-tips, plastic cup.

A cup with a lid that has an opening to insert a straw is a great tool for a dropping activity. A toddler can insert q-tips, pencils, or craft sticks. If the cup is clear, a child can watch the objects fall and stay there, which teaches object permanence.

Benefits: fine motor skills, hand eye coordination, grasping, development of concept of size and shape.

Flowers sensory play

Category: sensory play

Materials: flowers.

Toddlers are interested in everything around them. A bunch of flowers could become an early introduction to the aesthetics of nature. Toddlers can touch the flowers, smell them, shake them, take petals off some of them, and learn the correct names of the flowers. You can show your toddler how to arrange flowers in a vase. This activity should be watched to make sure the child doesn't eat any parts of the flower.

Benefits: motor skills, sensory play and general awareness of nature.

Pretend play

Category: intellectual development

Materials: toys, spoons, plates, cups.

Pretend play is a great activity for toddlers to learn social skills and compassion. Provide your toddler with spoons, plates, and cups and show how to feed animals and make eating sounds. Our toddler loves running around with a cup and a spoon trying to feed everything and everyone around her. Some other ideas for pretend play include putting an animal to sleep, singing to it, rocking it, taking it for a walk, taking it for a ride in a car, giving it a bath, brushing its teeth, etc.

Benefits: social skills, imagination, communication, emotional development, creativity.

Crunchy box

Materials: tray, cereal/noodles, play hammer/lemon squeezer.

You can use cereal, ramen noodles, popcorn, and a play hammer to crunch items in a tray. We used ramen noodles that I broke up apart in advance and a lemon squeezer instead of a hammer. This activity is great for satisfying toddler's curiosity and for releasing their energy.

Benefits: sensory awareness, introduction to concept of weight, hand coordination.

Thank you

Thank you for reading this book! I hope you found some activities your toddler enjoyed! By purchasing this book, you are encouraging me to spend more time on researching and creating kids' activities and I will be glad share them! Also, feel free to join our mailing list at www.chicklink.com/signup to be notified when the next book comes out or when the new posts on my blog are published.